Poems
for the
Journey

Poems
for the
Journey

CHRISTINA
WATKINS

Matchstick Literary
1-888-306-8885
orders@matchliterary.com

To David

To Dorene and Bruce
We loved getting to know
you and staying in your
beautiful guest house.
I hope you enjoy the poems.
CW

christinawatkinspoems.com

Contents

MEMORIAL SERVICE

MARY LUKE TOBIN

May 16, 1908
August 24, 2006

St. Mary's Academy
Englewood, Colorado

October 16, 2006

Travelling with Sister Mary Luke Tobin

Mary Luke and I were out together browsing
in bookstores, talking and telling stories.
Driving west towards white clouds streaked with gray
above the snow-capped blue on bluer Colorado mountains,
we saw a flock of starlings swoop like music in the sky before us.
We both said "Oh!"
Then there was silence.

As we drove the quiet highway into evening, in soft low tones,
she began to tell the story:
"Not long ago a priest died here in Denver.
He died of AIDS.
The funeral was last week so I and some other sisters went together.
There was a crowd because, you know, he was beloved.
The story I'm going to tell you now was given as the eulogy.

Six months before the young priest died
his order sent out someone unknown to him
to be his friend in dying and then to give his eulogy,
where he spoke of the last ravaging stages of AIDS and
the way the two went about in that community of suffering.
Together they learned to manage those last days.
Again and again people asked the friend if the two were lovers.

Twice he answered that it was friendship only.
He told of how they'd prayed and cried and said the rosary together.
When the question came a third time -- he answered softly --
as if he'd heard another sound.
'Yes' he said. 'In truth, that's what we were, lovers.'
That was how the funeral ended."
Mary Luke and I continued down the quiet road together.

Christina Watkins

Like Light In Running Water

At beach fires on Lake Erie my grandfather
fed chocolate cake to all children who gathered.
He smiled when he looked into their faces.

I did not know then
the fiery wall and water
that lead into paradise.

He was familiar with fire --.
the eldest son with brothers.
At some point he turned his face towards hope

left Perth in stony Lanark County for
southern Ontario's roses
became a doctor and married for love.

When the Great War came he signed on
with lines of men who dined like family
and then were empty places at the table.

In the dust of what is now Iraq
decked out in full camouflage--
he hid two nights in a shrub

until he killed the sniper
who had picked off his friends --
brothers under his command.

This tells the story that he --
a cardiologist-- stopped
the heart of a stranger.

Art on the walls
in my grandparents' home
hinted at the larger story.

A large engraved Indian brass tray,
carved by a murderer
rested on the fireplace mantle.

An oil in delicate golden hues
dreamed an Indian city
across a stretch of water.

These were gifts from friends he'd helped
in some medical way while visiting in Indian prisons.
He said he had not helped them out of duty.

As far now from my own childhood
as he was from his when I knew him best --
my grandfather's fire lives in my memory
like light in running water.

Christina Watkins

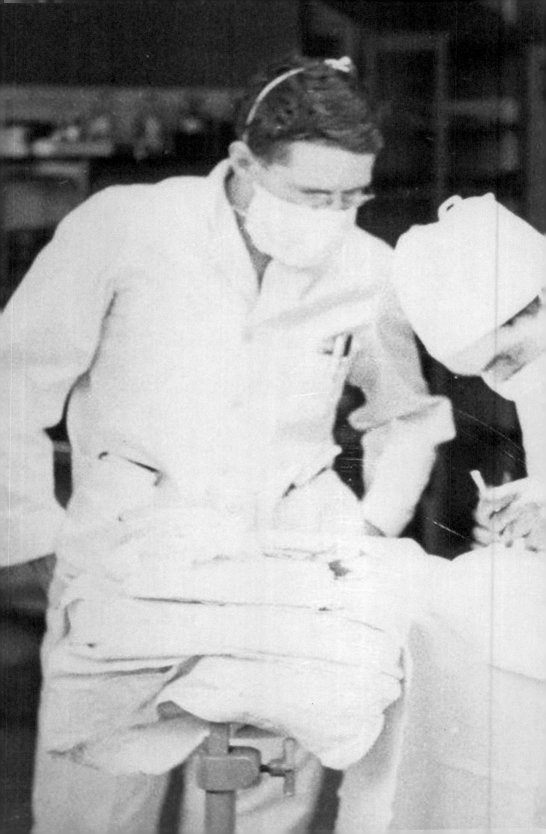

My Father's Hands

Now, many years after his death
I remember his hands as well as I remember his face.
The earliest story I recall of him is of
my four-year-old feisty self's insistence
that only my father take out the stitches in my abdomen
because he was best at not hurting.
It is true that he never struck me with his hands --
although -- from severe silence and strictness
I often felt bruised and sore.
He mended his hunting clothes and several times I watched
his long white slender fingers fold and open and
glide with the beauty of birds as they placed the needle
and pulled it through the khaki cloth.
At his funeral, three people told me that when
my father had examined them in hospital
he first moved his hands over their wounded parts
some inches from where their bodies seemed to start.
Then I knew that he knew how much larger we are than we seem to be.
Several months after his death, I saw him -- in a dream –
as he was wheeled down the hall on a gurney
by some of the surgeons he'd trained.
He had called them, his 'boys.'
He grinned and waved his right hand to me in friendship.
Then I began to claim the strength in my own hands.

Christina Watkins

To My Mother

Could we talk about the garden
while we have another day?
Do the roses need more pruning should the chairs be put away should
we speak about next summer though I know you cannot stay do forget-
me-nots need water

should I water every day? I've always meant to ask you what you wanted
me to plant in the corner by the fence where the sunshine's rather scant.
More lovely border flowers

or are the wild ones best? But you really needn't tell me for I see you
need to rest. And you've shown us very well all that you know best. So
rest now Mother rest.

Christina Watkins

Rory and Christine at Port.

Waves

A photograph of me and my eldest brother when we were young
shows one wild moment on the shore of Lake Erie
as I run in and he leaps out of the same wave.
Through the camera's hawk-eye time and space collapse.
Down the black and white portal decades disappear
until I feel again that glad radiance.

Wearing only bathing suits and our radiance
we lived long days, building castles, being young.
As afternoon sifted into evening, bright light disappeared.
We dreamed while moonlight shone a path on Lake Erie.
Night turned again to day in a soft collapse
as we heard the shore-line wave by wave.

Days and nights shortened. We gave a careless wave
to deep velvet darkness and golden radiance.
The realm of everlasting started to collapse
into ways of being that were no longer young.
Dead fish washed up on the shores of Lake Erie.
For us, running in and leaping out disappeared.

Warmth more and more disappeared.
Story gave way to cold hard facts, wave by wave.
In the dark we began to notice what was eerie.
After dreaming, we remembered less of radiance
'til it was hard to remember we had ever been young.
Possibilities of running in and leaping out collapsed.

Something partly understood engendered more collapse
while solitude grew and loneliness disappeared.
We again dared to believe the world was young.
At times we raggedly rode a wide wave
through sparkling waters bathed in radiance.
The fish were swimming again in Lake Erie.

Our family no longer summers on Lake Erie.
Rhythms of generations have collapsed
into increasing circles of new radiance.
Through death some dear ones have disappeared
into an unknown yet near holy wave
that moves beyond what we know of old and young.

Christina Watkins

Diamonds and Sutras

Some people make their fortunes finding diamonds.
Others practice knowledge of the *sutras*.
Everyone loves listening to stories.
Many forget their worries while watching baseball.
I wonder how we all live into surrender
know that all shall be well beyond space and time.

In a game with rules and the mystery of time-
out, in an open field shaped like a diamond,
to play together requires a kind of surrender.
Commentary for this could be based on the *sutras*.
Long afternoons richly spent focused on baseball
bring on dreams and become the stuff of stories.

From the beginning I read our children stories.
Those were the final innings of every bedtime.
My own childhood was enriched by the game of baseball.
It was lovely to spend that time focused on diamonds.
Now I'm writing poems and reading the *sutras*.
Batting and running help to balance surrender.

Lack of balance leads to uncentered surrender.
Practice and play take us home again to our stories.
Some things can be explained best through *sutras*.
A practice of love is active over time.
Many assume that all of us are diamonds.
Groups of three can remind us of more than baseball.

Evenings spent under the stars watching baseball –
with overtime the splendid surrender
to freedom from clocks -- a treat as rare as diamonds --
replay in my heart as memory that now is story.
One day I'll write a poem about the time
when 'It ain't over till it's over' became my *sutra*.

Playing is more precious even than *sutras*.
Plenty has come to me through games like baseball.
Nothing moves more relentlessly than time.
Now I gather my strength for what seems like surrender
while praying and paying close attention to stories
about lives of fire and ice brighter than diamonds.

Our grandchildren now play baseball games on diamonds.
We make up sutras to help them with surrender --
enrichment for us and our stories over time.

Christina Watkins

The Way Things Are Is Large

The way things are is large, too wonderful to understand.
Love teaches by story, portrays our needs.
But what is it that makes us human?

Story tells of a garden, suggests a plan.
We learn which are flowers, are warned of weeds.
The way things are is large, too wonderful to understand.

We hear more stories, the collection is grand,
tales of flood and drought, of gift and greed.
But what is it that makes us human?

With myriad creatures, we share the land.
In hopes and hungers we seek what we need.
The way things are is large, too wonderful to understand.

The garden is a mix of loam, weeds and sand.
From above come sun, rain and seeds.
But what is it that makes us human?

One story says a time will come for outstretched hands,
a part of the path where we follow another's lead.
The way things are is large, too wonderful to understand.
What is it that makes us human?

Christina Watkins

One Snowy Afternoon

I cross country skied in South Porcupine
when eyelashes clumped white from the cold.
At three o'clock the babysitter mercifully arrived
and stayed till night began to fall around four.
In colorful breathable light layers of clothes
I skied across the road and field into
woods that stretched all the way up to James Bay.

After a property dispute about sharing toys
I was weary – winter was long.
I skied fast -- so lost in thought that
I failed to notice the snow beginning to fall.
I saw my covered tracks. I was lost.
Light was slant as I skied past trees I didn't know --
circling – passing the same ones again and again.

Then there was a shift in my vision into light.
Hope sprang up deep and wide.
I heard the sound of teenagers talking.
As I cried and laughed I skied towards them.

From that road where we lived-- after
night had fully fallen -- we sometimes
saw the glorious dancing Aurora Borealis,
the northern lights.

Is there something about light dancing
that leads us back to inner times
when light has broken us open?

Christina Watkins

There Is An Opening, A Door

There is an opening, a door.
When we find it we may go through
to where the more is more
of truth that lies beneath disguise

What's false goes tumbling to the floor.
All that remains we know as You.
Under the guise of weak and poor
You are the truth that's good and wise.

Disguises lead us more and more
to all that shines as something new.
The treasure that's disguised as poor
is joy that takes us by surprise.

Christina Watkins

The Mexican Jaguar

Early days in Sonora
I went by jeep and bony backed mules
with my husband to a field camp.
The eight Mexicans there were shy as
we said Buenos Dias to each other.
Next morning they answered my Buenos Días
with Buenos Días del Diós.
It became like that.

I stayed in camp all day while
they went out to hammer rocks in the barranca –
a place of broken boulders.
My husband and I slept that night in
the small cook shack.
The Mexicans in sleeping bags
circled close round the fire.

Next morning fear was in the camp.
We heard the words gato – cat and pero– dog
and a word we did not know --ónca.
The Mexicans said I must not be left alone.
We thought gato meant lynx-like.

That night the Mexicans stayed up late talking.
In the morning the second dog was gone.
Ignoring anxious warnings from the Mexicans
I stayed in camp reading by the river.

After lunch -- to the relief of the Mexicans --
my husband and I went back to our town
by bony backed mules and jeep.

Years later-- in Tucson's Desert Museum-
we saw a sign saying Ónca.
We turned a corner towards it -- then
suddenly faced a brown, black and gold
Painted Jaguar --
huge and confident looking.
I felt my full foolishness.

Those Mexicans in that long ago camp --
wanted me safe – in spite of myself.
They were my blessing.

Christina Watkins

Pomegranate Seeds

In the years when I was young
often in September my mother bought one
pomegranate to share with me.
Did she wonder then if my life would be like her life?
One wintry season when she was thirteen
her mother died of sleeping sickness.

I saw in her parent's home a painting of Demeter and Persephone.
The young and older women's fingers stretched towards each other in
the grey light.
The same pinks and blues of their faces cool as earth
reflected the foreground as loving yearning.
Near this larger painting which hung above a blue sofa was
a cherubic painting of my mother, aged three.

One September I married and moved to the far side of the world.
I slept while my mother was awake and then woke as she slept.
Every year I made my way back to her from time-zones
climates and cultures different from those she had known.
Deeply and lightly we mothered and daughtered each other till
one September day my mother passed into the larger season.

In autumns when I am far from my own daughters I eat pomegranate seeds.
I eat the fruit in juicy tender chicken dishes.
I drink the bright juice mixed with sparkling lightly sugared water.
I write this for my mother
for my daughters and granddaughter --
for everyone who loves – and knows yearning.

Christina Watkins

Calling

Lately
I notice birds on branches
calling softly to me,
"Come closer, come over, come in."
I'm here.

Christina Watkins

Christina Watkins lives with her husband
in Victoria, British Columbia, Canada

Reviews

"I've always been a fan of books of poems about life experiences. I think her main goal is to connect with others and share different experiences of life with other readers just like you..."

"This book serves as a beautiful companion on your journey in life..."

"The poems touched the inner depths of my soul and my self-esteem boosted. I was able to appreciate how important it is to have personal growth."

CPSIA information can be obtained
at www.ICGtesting.com
Printed in the USA
BVHW061933060521
606610BV00001B/3